That Time a Fish Loved a Bird

Lee Gray

Published by Lee Gray, 2018.

While every precaution has been taken in the preparation of this book, the publisher assumes no responsibility for errors or omissions, or for damages resulting from the use of the information contained herein.

THAT TIME A FISH LOVED A BIRD

First edition. October 31, 2018.

Copyright © 2018 Lee Gray.

ISBN: 979-8201763749

Written by Lee Gray.

Also by Lee Gray

That Time a Fish Loved a Bird
Shit I'm Tired of Saying
What They Didn't Teach Yo Ass in School
All That is Love
She is (not) my King

Watch for more at https://www.instagram.com/leegpoet/.

For Olivia.

Bigger Than, Greater Than You

Men spend their lives
balding,
worrying about size,
while women orgasm
with two fingers
and trembling thighs.

Crush

Everyday
unaware,
she undones me,
ravishes my insides,
turns my heart,
until I can not move,
can not breathe
for want of her.
And she doesn't know.
Doesn't see me.
Can not see me,
this shy and shadowy night
lurking on the edge of her blinding light.

Dear Self

Let me love you.
Let me place warm petals
of kisses
where it aches.
Let me hold your hand
and lift your chin
when you can't stand.
Let me dare to look at your reflection and say
"I love you"
again and again
without shame.

Homophobes

We were flowers
standing side by side
in the dark.
Stiffly silent in our beauty and lust.
Unable to touch each other,
unable to glance,
for fear
of the gardener's
shears.

Mermaid Ashore

I am a mermaid
swamped in sand
with mud and blood
upon my crown.
By lust
unmoved,
unashamed,
they *stare*.
As in the air
I slowly drown.

I Stand

Each day it hurts
as I sew myself back together.
Blood
runs in rivulets
from the teeth of your hate.
But I stand.
Pieces puzzled together.
Frail.
And barely held with duct tape.
I stand.

Mirror

"I love you."
Can you
look in the mirror
and say those words
without tears?

Self-Love

There is no manual
to the human heart.
Just puzzle it together.
A Band-Aid over this crack here.
Stitches to hold those pieces there.
Pet your own hair.
Be gentle with yourself.
Write love letters to you.
Good thoughts. Happy place.
You are wonderful.
You are beautiful.
You are worthy.
Fill your own cup
until it overflows
and spills
into someone else's heart.

She is the Sun

Her eyes
are watery hazel mirrors—
gold when absorbing the light.
Long blonde hair
like ribbons of bright day.
She is the sun,
eclipsing my night.

Glory

Can you forgive yourself
for not being perfect?
Can you let yourself just be?
There is nothing to forgive.
You weren't supposed to be perfect.
You were just supposed
to be.
In all your
pimply, lopsided, chaffed, stretchmarked
glory.

O

Oh
to spread the lips
of her dewy flower
and taste
the rich dark
petals.

She, I

She, I,
was too young to put a name to it.
To the hatred of all things She.
She, I,
grew anyway,
loved anyway,
thought anyway,
kissed anyway,
learned anyway,
danced anyway,
breathed anyway.
Hate only fuels
the fire
of unapologetic defiance.

Still the Sun

You are the sun
and I the night—
shadowy and shy,
yet longing to bathe
in your fiery light.

Tonight

I dream of her strong arms
consuming me
as night consumes the sky—
a slow seduction.
Sweetly slipping
its fingers
through the warm pubic nest
of daylight's
dewy hair.

Alive

I thought I was dead and numb,
that there was nothing left.
And then her eyes.
Her eyes looked into my soul
without even seeing me,
without knowing that I gazed back.
A wisp of flame licked to life inside me,
narrow in the dark,
but roaring all the same.
And the life spilled from my loins,
as only a woman's loins can spill:
wet and wild and wanting.
Music sang in my words,
whispers she will never hear . . .
kisses she will never feel.

Cup Runneth Over

I had so much love to give
and no one to give it to.
So I gave it
to myself.

Thief

They hand me a basket
to keep my hands busy.
As if I had no intention
of busying myself with buying.
They follow me
from shelf to shelf,
from aisle to aisle,
ever watching.
Every gesture,
every purse search,
every pocket rifle
is suspect.
They do not know
that my soul sings poetry.
They do not know
that I paint red skies of joy.
They do not know
I am a mermaid,
walking on sand,
my erstwhile tail forgotten for land.
They do not know
I am a person.
I could walk in the store naked,
but I can not unclothe my skin,
my nose,
my nappy hair.
My skin,
my nose,
my nappy hair
was all they saw in the first place.

I Miss Her

Only recently did I realize.
Whenever I was on a ledge,
she was always at my side,
standing there,
ready to pull me back to safety.
So consumed was I by grief,
I did not feel her invisible hands,
nor see the footprints in the sand beside my own
that belonged to no one.

I Am Woman

Being a woman feels like
always having –
"Wait, let me, a man, explain womanhood to you—!"
—Always having someone speak over me.
It feels like
my father's friend
when I'm sixteen
commenting on how pretty I am
with lust in his eyes.
It feels like
having a strange man
eye-fuck my tits
at the grocery store
for ten minutes
regardless of how visibly pissed and uncomfortable I am.
It feels like
the constant fear
of getting my period
at school,
of having that line of red
run down my leg
during gym class.
It feels like
using tampons that hurt me
because they are made by men,
who think women walk around
constantly wet and aroused,
men who have nothing but a sexualized notion
of a vagina.
It feels like

being raped
and having people tell me
what I should have done
to have avoided it.
It feels like
being elven years old,
developing breasts,
and wearing baggy clothes
to hide my body
just to avoid unwanted comments
and stares
from men twice my age.
It feels like
crossing to the other side of the street
to avoid a group of men
who will stop to stare
and shout disgusting things
should I walk within twenty feet of them.
It feels like
constantly being groped in high school,
suffering forced kisses and hugs from teenage boys,
having teachers tell me I'm mean for hitting my assailants,
being shamed for my anger,
being told not to fight back.
It feels like
hearing everyday
for my entire life
how men are owed my
time
space
smile
touch

kiss
kind word
listening ear
body.
It feels like
being treated like a thing,
like a decoration
that exists solely
to make men hard.
It feels like
being called a
"bitch"
"slut"
"whore"
"cunt"
for having some agency,
for making a choice,
for having a boundary,
for saying "No."
It feels like
earning less money for the same job men do.
It feels like
having my serious problems
belittled daily
to the point that my own healthcare
can kill me.
It feels like
having every space for women
invaded by men
until there is no place on the planet
where I can be free from
catcalls,

slurs,
leering,
groping,
flashing,
forced kisses,
forced hugs,
forced touching,
the insistence that I must want dick,
the violent tantrums of men
who think they are not to be denied,
who think I exist for them,
who see me not as a person
but as a thing to be acquired
through a series of
the "right" words
and
the "right" actions.
It feels like
assault masquerading as feminism.
It feels like
having someone
refer to my entire sex
as "tits and ass"
while men as a group are never referred to entirely as
"cocks and balls."
It feels like
dehumanization.
It feels like
never seeing myself
depicted as anything more than a sex object
in any media
anywhere

ever.
Not even a damn Burger King commercial.
It feels like
rage.
It feels like
fire.
It feels like
a thousand furious winds
welling up inside,
beating against my ribcage
every time a man assumes
I dressed myself for him,
assumes that this warrants
comments and stares.
It feels like
a boot on my neck.
It feels like . . .
You know what?
It doesn't "feel" like a damn thing.
"Woman" is not a feeling.
"Woman" is not an identity.
"Woman" is not a choice.
I don't "feel" like a woman.
I *am* a woman.

The Wanting

It used to be
I would lie awake,
soul aching,
unable to sleep for sadness.
Now I lie awake,
soul aching,
unable to sleep for want of you.
How do I undo this?
Uncast this spell?
Unbuckle
the buckling
of my knees?
Release me,
I beg of you.
Never release me . . .
I beg of you.

My Soul Awoke

My soul awoke
when it laid eyes on her.
And how it ached.
How it stirred.
The wild want
beating in my breast.
My soul screamed
and knew no rest.

Be Careful

Be careful
baring your
candy soul to me.
I may turn you inside-out,
and lick your wrapper clean.

A Poet

To be a poet
means you carry
tremendous pain on your shoulders,
a stone around your neck,
needles under your skin,
the scars of careless lovers
across every curve.
It means
you can no longer stand
your own silence.

Cocoon

I'm just a caterpillar.
Wait until I'm a butterfly.
Wait until I
can shower you
with all the affection
you so richly deserve.
Wait
for picnics by the sand
restaurants
museums
sunny vacations
trips to Disney Land.
Wait
for little surprises,
gifts, presents, precious favors
around every corner,
behind every door.
Wait
until I am worthy enough
to give you
so much more.

Majesty

Never stop believing
in your own majesty.
You are mighty.
You are a mountain
rising vast above the land.
Unmovable.
Unshakable.
Unbreakable.
And they can not
bring you down.

Art Gallery

I don't want to sell my art.
How many times
must I cut myself into pieces
for someone else's
pleasure?

Lips

Yours is
quite a stubborn mouth.
You know,
I dream of kissing your lips . . .
and then kissing your lips.

Distance

I feel you sometimes,
wondering.
Feel the flower of your cool and pensive mind
unfold within my own.
I'm still here.
Can't you feel my soul
and how it aches for you?
And only you.

Not Alone

You are not alone.
You are not in the dark.
You are simply blinded by your own light.

Body and Soul

You don't like me.
You like my breasts.
You don't want to have sex with me.
You want to have sex with my body.
I am not even here.
I am not a person to you.
I am something to consume.
Something to be taken,
conquered,
coerced,
coaxed.
Another quiet triumph.
Another scratched off tick.
A thing used to uplift you.
It doesn't register in your mind,
the violation,
the destruction of a human being,
in your quest to rise.

Mother

I don't hate you on purpose.
You put that hate in me.
Recited it to me everyday with words that cut like knives.
And like most children,
I didn't question your furious flame.
I accepted it.
Took it deep inside.
Let it simmer for all my life.
And then one day when I was grown,
the flame burst out of me,
piercing through tongue, teeth, and eyes.
Do you have any reason
to be so surprised?

Ugly

I reflect,
the way water reflects the moon,
hoping to imitate her quiet beauty
and ceaseless serenity.

Lost

How did you get here?
To a place without roads?
To a place without signs
or people
or love?

No one Cares

How do you forgive someone?
I don't know.
I don't know.
Instead I hold on to the rage,
no matter how it burns my hands,
until it has consumed us both,
and our world is a bitter wasteland
of skeletons and ash,
cracked earth and bleeding walls.
And even long after we are standing in the dust,
still I rage.
Still I rage.
Believing no one can hear me
in my unending need
to be heard.
To be seen.
Believing no one cares
that you made me bleed.

Free Things

In my youth
I gave my love away,
thinking someone would give theirs freely in return.
But like all free things,
my love was unvalued,
taken for granted,
thrown by the wayside,
tossed in the garbage
like a wad of used tissue.
I picked up my love,
smoothed her crinkles,
gave her away again,
thinking, "Surely, this time."
But not this time.
Nor the next.
Now my precious love
is in a safe.
Waiting in the dark
for the person
with the right key.

Don't Touch Me

Don't let the sundress fool you.
My combat boots will crush your soul.
My words will break your bones.
And I have a knee-jerk reaction
where people
fly through walls.

Infinite You

You are music.
You are a masterpiece.
A symphony of muscles and sinew.
An intricate ticking clock,
ever churning, turning,
flexing,
and unaware
of all the little workers inside you
that scramble daily to move you.
You breathe.
You laugh.
You live.
Unknowing
of the sheer force within.
That a fragment of the immortal
breathes within your skin.

Nail Polish

I am not soft.
I am merely hiding
how hard
and jaded
and recklessly wild I am.
I am a wolf,
prowling in iridescent moonlight.
I am a lioness,
cloaked by endless fields of glittering gold.
I am a tigress,
swathed in brilliant orange,
unbothered by you unless my belly growls,
ready to swat you down
should you have the foolish audacity
to rise to me.

I Miss You

And I don't even know you.
But it seems you should be here.
Like I have known your arms before
and your kisses on my hair.
And your smile.
And the way your body moves
when you are sleeping,
breasts rising with your breaths,
and all the world is still
as the night winds my heart tighter to yours.

Save That Kiss

Would you save your kiss for me,
sweetheart?
Save your kiss for me.
Don't let any woman kiss
your stubborn mouth.
Don't let any woman hold
your baller's hands.
Don't let any woman sit
upon that lap.
I know my breasts, my body
would fill the space between your arms,
would fill your baller's hands,
perfectly.

I Crave You

The way the dry earth craves water.
The way life craves air.
It is incessant, the craving,
driving me to distraction during the day,
invading my dreams in the night.
I thought I could ignore it.
Might as well ignore my own skin.
It is there,
forever touching me . . .
so deep within.

This Must Be

This must be
what the love songs are about,
the poems,
all the sappy sonnets.
When I think of your eyes
the world stands still,
unmoving,
as stricken as I.
Unable to speak,
unable to breathe,
as body struggles to reconnect with brain.
This must be
what "smitten" means.

She

She
lit a flame
and left it to burn in me.
Stood back and watched
as I was consumed.
Waited to see
if the fire would linger.
And how I suffered,
longing to pull her
into the flames
and let them ravish us both.

Work to Do

Someone told me the spirits could not help unless I asked.
And I realized I didn't remember how to ask,
that it had been beaten out of me,
my inner child silenced,
disconnected from light,
life,
and from my own magic.
Conjuration at my fingertips,
but too down in the dark to see it.
I had forgotten how to pray –
could not speak the words,
resented Them for abandoning me . . .
when it was I who abandoned Them.
"Now you remember who you are," They said,
"Will you give up? Will you come home now?"
"No," I answered,
"I still have work to do here."

The Mystery of Me

She wonders.
She wonders where I am,
though I am so very close,
our souls entwined,
our hearts bound,
our minds ever linking.
You wonder.
You wonder at the mystery of me.
But if you find me
will you like what you see?
Or will you have grown accustomed
to the face you created for me?

Move the Earth

Let us come together
and make the very stars explode,
bring the heavens shattering down,
leave the mountains torn and weeping.
We will melt inside each other
and in the morning
wake
drowsy and content.

Look

You've unraveled me.
I am putty at your feet
and praying
you don't walk through
my puddle.

Stop

People ask why there are so many gay poets.
Stop
giving us
something to write about,
and we'll stop writing poetry.
(Maybe.)

A Fish

I am
a Fish who glanced up
and loved a Bird.
Knew I would never
fit into her nest.
Knew I would never
grow wings to reach her.
But loved her still.

No More Words

Let me sit now in silence
and bask in your beauty.
You have taken all the words.
There are no more words.

Did you love *That Time a Fish Loved a Bird*? Then you should read *All That is Love*[1] by Lee Gray!

A collection of poems musing on the realities of unconditional, romantic love.

Read more at https://www.instagram.com/leegpoet/.

---

1. https://books2read.com/u/mlrgqZ

2. https://books2read.com/u/mlrgqZ

About the Author

Lee is a lesbian who lives in California.
Read more at https://www.instagram.com/leegpoet/.